NPL F
Nashville Public Library | FOUNDATION

*This book given
to the Nashville Public Library
through the generosity of the*
***Dollar General
Literacy Foundation***

WHY SHOULD I CARE ABOUT THE ANCIENT CHINESE?

By Claire Throp

Consultant
Michael Wert
Associate Professor
Marquette University
Milwaukee, WI

COMPASS POINT BOOKS
a capstone imprint

Why Should I Care About History? is published by Compass Point Books,
an imprint of Capstone.
1710 Roe Crest Drive, North Mankato, Minnesota 56003
www.capstonepub.com

**Library of Congress Cataloging-in-Publication Data is available on the Library
of Congress website.**
ISBN: 978-0-7565-6424-7 (library binding)
ISBN: 978-0-7565-6566-4 (paperback)
ISBN: 978-0-7565-6425-4 (eBook PDF)

Summary: From pasta to paper, the inventions of the ancient Chinese remain
part of everyday life in our modern world. Learn how items like wheelbarrows,
the first toothbrushes, and early earthquake detectors have evolved into devices
we know today and discover just how big of an impact the ancient Chinese have
had on your life.

Photo Credits:
Alamy; Chronicle, 54, Lou-Foto, 58, The Protected Art Archive, 46, Wilawan
Khasawong, 41; Newscom: British Library/Album, 16, 18, FeatureChina/Liu
Tao, 20 (bottom), Image China, 8, Li Yibo Xinhua News Agency, 13, Zhuang
Yingchang Xinhua News Agency, 20 (top); Shutterstock: chung toan co, 29,
Elena11, 23, Everett Historical, 19, Harvepino, 45, hjochen, 51, Jade ThaiCatwalk,
32, Jixin YU, 28, Louis W., 27, Mahno Uhnseni, 35, Marzolino, 43, milart, 53,
MING-HSIANG, 26, Naurora, 48, New Africa, 49, NOPPHARAT STUDIO 969,
37, nuu_jeed, 25, phototr, 9, OSTILL is Franck Camhi, Cover (right), tratong,
Cover (left), Wantanee Chantasilp, 10, www.sandatlas.org, 40, yeo2205, 15;
The Image Works, 21; XNR Productions, 6

Design Elements:
Shutterstock: Artem Kovalenco

Editorial Credits:
Editor: Gina Kammer; Designer: Tracy McCabe; Media Researcher: Jo Miller;
Production Specialist: Laura Manthe

Printed and bound in the United States of America.
PA99

TABLE OF CONTENTS

CHAPTER 1

WAY TO RULE!: DYNASTIES TO REPUBLIC

Have you ever wondered who invented the brilliant fireworks you saw on Independence Day last year? Or who developed those straight roads we drive on? What about all those theories in math that you study at school? Many of the items that we regularly enjoy, use, or learn about today were invented in ancient times.

The ancient Chinese invented many different things that are part of our everyday lives. The "big four" refers to inventions and techniques that are considered to be the most important and influential. They are paper, printing, gunpowder, and the magnetic compass.

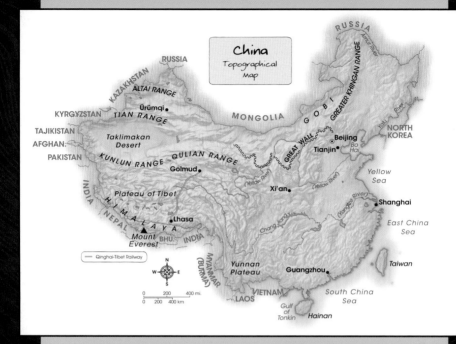

The Yellow River is one of the longest rivers in the world. Mount Everest in the Himalayas is the highest mountain in the world. The Plateau of Tibet is the world's largest. Deserts, plains, and basins also make up the vast country.

WHO WERE THE ANCIENT CHINESE, ANYWAY?

China is a huge country about the size of the United States. The country has a vastly diverse geography. There are mountain ranges to the west and huge deserts to the north. A tropical rain forest borders the south and the Pacific Ocean to the east.

More than 6,000 years ago, the first Chinese civilizations formed. They sprouted up along the Yellow River because of the fertile land there. The following period, starting about 4,000 years ago, is known as the Xia. But not much is known about these early civilizations. The Shang dynasty (1600 to 1046 BC) is the first period we really know anything about. This is because picture writing appeared during this time.

From the Shang onward, these first dynasties—or ruling families—governed ancient China. The Chinese Empire is the longest continuous civilization in the world. It began in 221 BC, when it was set up by the first emperor, and ended in 1912, when the last emperor was overthrown.

FACT

The Yellow River, also called the Huang He, is 3,395 miles (5,464 kilometers) long. It is the second-longest river in China. Part of the river often floods, so it has been called "China's Sorrow."

WAY TO RULE ... AN EMPIRE!

Like many countries around the world today, China has a civil service. The civil service includes the people responsible for the day-to-day running of the country. They work for the government. People get civil service jobs by taking an exam or being interviewed. In ancient China, the civil service was set up by Gaozu, the first emperor of the Han dynasty (206 BC–AD 220). Gaozu was not an educated man. But he realized that in order to keep the Chinese Empire running smoothly, he would need educated people. He put them in charge of public services such as schools and taxes. This system allowed the vast empire to be ruled efficiently. The ancient Chinese had to take an extremely difficult exam in order to get into the civil service. This was so that the best

The civil service examinations were conducted at every level of Chinese administration. The fourth and highest level of examinations were given in the palace itself. Today, the National Civil Service Exam is a highly competitive exam taken to enter government jobs.

We can thank the ancient Chinese for inventing the fireworks used in our different festivities today. Fireworks were even used in the very first U.S. Independence Day celebration.

people would get the jobs. This was very different from other governments throughout history. Top jobs would go to people who owned land or were wealthy. But they were not necessarily the best people for the job. Gaozu was ahead of his time!

WHY SO MANY INVENTIONS?

Ancient China had a very stable social structure. This was partly because of those smart civil servants running the government so well. Ideas such as those

set out by a man known as Confucius helped too. His philosophy encouraged the Chinese people to live a family-centered life, and focused on education and respect for others.

Also, for most of the Chinese Empire's history, it was peaceful. This was unlike Europe, where countries spent a lot of time and money fighting each other, leaving little time to be creative. Ancient China, on the other hand, produced many amazing inventions.

Most common Chinese people knew very little of the rest of the world outside of East Asia. Their location helped to encourage original ideas and discoveries. And some of those inventions and developments have had a huge effect in our lives.

DYNASTIES IN ANCIENT CHINA	
Shang	1600–1046 BC
Zhou	1027–256 BC
Warring States Period	481–221 BC
Qin	221–207 BC
Han	206 BC – AD 220
Period of Disunity	AD 221–589
Sui	589–618
Tang	618–906
Five Dynasties	907–960
Song	960–1279
Yuan	1279–1368
Ming	1368–1644
Qing	1644–1912

CHAPTER 2

A PRESSING NEED FOR PAPER AND PRINTING

How many times a day do you come into contact with paper? Think about the sticky notes, paper bags, wrapping paper, cards, and books you often see. While we now try to use less paper for environmental reasons, it is still in widespread use. Paper and printing are two of the most important inventions to come from the ancient Chinese.

A form of paper was created by the ancient Egyptians. However, the sort of paper that is more recognizable to us today was developed by the ancient Chinese. Paper was invented in the 2nd century BC. It was originally used as wrapping paper, not writing paper. Paper was used to wrap medicines, which we know because of an ancient paper that has been found with the names of medicines

written on it. Apparently, in 12 BC, a person even used poison that was wrapped in paper to commit murder!

PAPER MADE FROM WHAT?

Cai Lun (AD 62–121) was a Chinese court official. He is usually credited with perfecting the papermaking process. In AD 105, he formed sheets of paper using tree bark, hemp waste, rags, and fishing nets. This paper was easier to write on than silk—which was in common use at the time—and also cheaper to produce. Cai Lun's apprentice, Zuo Bo, later invented a process to make paper whiter and smoother by forcing it through two heavy rollers called calenders.

During the Eastern Jin dynasty (AD 317–420), paper production increased with lots of new types of paper developed including moss, vine, and bamboo paper. This paper was traded using the Silk Roads to the Islamic world, including Iraq and Iran, in the 700s. It was then passed on to Europe via Sicily and Spain. Only from the 1300s did people north of the Alps make their own paper. Until then, it was imported from China.

Paper has had a huge effect on the world. Unlike parchment, leather, and other materials used for writing on, paper absorbs ink. So it could be used for printing. The printing revolution could not have taken place without paper. Cheaper books could be printed. Therefore, more people could afford books, which meant education levels rose. Information, news, and culture could spread wider and quicker.

EDUCATION

For many children in the ancient world, education simply meant following in their parents' footsteps. If a boy's father was a farmer, then that's the job the boy learned to do. Boys in wealthier families had tutors and studied math as well as how to read and write Chinese characters. Girls were mainly taught music, painting, and how to get along with others. Even the girls who were taught more academic subjects were not allowed to take civil service exams. Those were strictly for boys.

Calligraphy is an art form—the art of writing. Chinese writing does not rely on representing sounds, such as in English. Each character is a one-of-a-kind symbol that represents a word. Yet the characters are more than words. They are also forms of beauty.

CALLIGRAPHY—WAY MORE THAN HANDWRITING

Have you ever doodled your name in fancy letters on a notebook? Maybe you have! Have you ever tried to find out the answers to questions by writing on a turtle shell and then heating it? Probably not! The ancient Chinese did, though. The earliest Chinese writing appeared on oracle bones during the Shang dynasty, around 1600–1046 BC. Oracle bones were used by people called

FACT

If you take the official Chinese language test, you need to show knowledge of 2,600 characters. But there are thousands more— possibly as many as 106,230!

Oracle bones contain China's oldest known writing. In the Shang dynasty (1600–1046 BC), a diviner listened to someone's questions. The diviner then carved symbols onto a bone, such as the shoulder blade of an ox. The bone was heated until it cracked. The diviner then interpreted the cracks as answers to the questions.

diviners. These diviners asked important questions about the future. They then heated the bones of an ox or the shell of a turtle and "read" the cracks that appeared as answers to their questions. Eventually, this early form of writing developed into Chinese script and calligraphy. Calligraphy, unlike our usual quickly scribbled notes, is more decorative. It's even considered an art.

Calligraphy means "beautiful writing." Chinese writing is very different from our own. It involves strokes or lines to create symbols or characters. There are many more characters—thousands, in fact—than the Western alphabet has letters. In China, calligraphy has been viewed as more important than works of art such as paintings or sculptures. The Chinese used sharp, pointed instruments to scratch the writing on oracle bones. Those were replaced by brush, ink, and paper during the Han dynasty (206 BC–AD 220).

Chinese writing has developed over the years and has now been simplified, coming a long way from etchings on turtle shells! But calligraphy is not just for communication. It has become popular around the world as an art form, as people see the beauty in calligraphy.

PRINTING MEETS MOVABLE TYPE

Where would we be without printing? Inventing paper was one thing, but without the means to print text, it had limited use. Think about how often you see printed words during the day in books, magazines, on menus, signs, instructions, or ingredients. Without printed materials, how difficult would it be to know what was in a food item if you have an allergy? How would you put together the model spaceship that you were given as a present?

German inventor Johannes Gutenberg is well known as the inventor of the printing press in 1439, but the Chinese invention of block printing came 800 years earlier. Text was carved into wooden blocks (in reverse so that it was printed the correct way). The blocks were then covered in ink and pressed onto paper. A text called *Diamond Sutra* is the first complete printed book from AD 868. It was discovered inside a cave near Dunhuang in 1900.

In the AD 1040s, a man named Bi Sheng improved the process by inventing movable type. He produced hundreds of individual characters. The characters were made from baked clay and placed in metal plates. Each page required a separate block. Ink was made from pine resin, wax, and paper ashes. Thousands of copies could be printed quickly. It took hundreds of years for this method to catch on, though. Part of the problem was that Chinese writing includes thousands of different characters.

The *Diamond Sutra* is a scroll of printed pages that extends more than 17 feet (5 meters) long. This "book" contains a Chinese translation of Buddhist teachings.

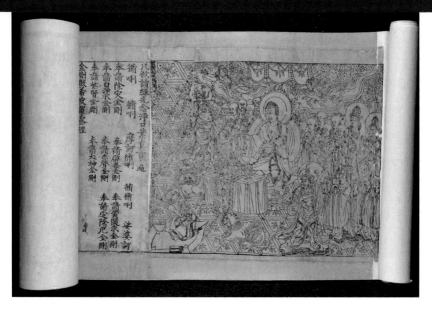

FURTHER PRINTING DEVELOPMENTS

Johannes Gutenberg invented the printing press in 1439. Until then, books in Europe were copied by hand. Mass production of books in Europe followed, including the Gutenberg Bible in 1455.

There have been many printing developments since, including new fonts, improved methods of production, newspapers, paperback books, and the list goes on.

Johannes Gutenberg's printing press used a mechanical process to ink the plates of movable type and press them to paper. The invention of the press made the use of movable type much more efficient and quick.

FACT

The Gutenberg Bible was called the Forty-Two-Line Bible because the Latin text was printed in columns that were each 42 lines long.

None of these would have been possible had the papermaking process not been perfected by Cai Lun and if Bi Sheng hadn't invented movable type. Thank you, ancient Chinese inventors!

The individual small character blocks had to be placed together in a plate to make up one page. But each plate could be inked many times for many copies.

A Yuan dynasty banknote from 1287 was printed with a metal plate. Paper money was first known to be used in China during the Tang dynasty (618–906). It wasn't until the Song dynasty (960–1279) that paper money was made official by the government.

PAPER MONEY

We're used to paying for goods with paper currency, but this system came as a shock to explorer Marco Polo in 1298. He was visiting China, and it was the first time he had ever seen paper money. It had first been created about 300 years earlier. But Polo was amazed by the idea that a piece of paper could be trusted by everyone to represent money simply because it had been signed by the emperor. Polo wrote a book telling of his travels through China. The chapter in which he described paper money was called "How the Great Khan [the emperor] Causes the Bark of Trees, Made into Something Like Paper, to Pass for Money All over His Country." Snappy title!

CHAPTER 3

NEW ON THE MENU—NOW SERVED WITH CHOPSTICKS!

Do you enjoy Chinese food or trying out chopsticks? You probably already know none of these things are new! The ancient Chinese led the way with their inventions and discoveries in the world of food and drink.

CH'A CHING!: THE HISTORY OF TEA

Tea is the second-most popular drink in the world, only behind water. Did you know that it was first used by the ancient Chinese as medicine to help digestion?

Shen Nung, the Chinese emperor in 2737 BC, was an herbalist. Legend has it that while waiting for his servant to boil some water, leaves from a tea plant fell and landed in the water. The emperor drank it, and from this accident came the start of the culture of tea drinking.

Tea containers have been found in tombs dating from the Han dynasty (206 BC–AD 220). By the time of the Tang dynasty (AD 618–906), tea was China's national drink. In the late 700s, Lu Yu even wrote a book entirely about tea, the *Ch'a Ching* (Tea Classic). In it, he gave detailed instructions for the best way to make tea. This was considered a valuable skill at the time.

After Lu Yu's book was published, some Japanese monks visited China and tried tea for the first time. They took it back to Japan where it became very popular. *Chadō*, means "the way of tea." It is a process in which the preparing and serving of green tea is used to help a person find a spiritual calm. The process can last for four hours!

TEA TRAVELS TO EUROPE

Merchants from the Dutch East India Company first imported tea into Europe. Tea became fashionable in Holland and this soon spread to other countries. Portugal's Catherine of Braganza, who became the wife of King Charles II in Britain, was a big tea fan. She inspired many Britons to start drinking tea in the late 1660s. Yes, people have been copying everything celebrities do for years!

Taxes placed on tea by the British later led to the American Revolutionary War. Taxes also led to a major smuggling trade in Britain as people tried to buy their tea at a cheaper price. Despite these issues, tea remained a very popular drink.

FACT

It is believed that drinking four cups of tea a day is the best amount to maintain your health.

ALONG CAME TEA BAGS

For most people today, drinking tea is a far easier process than it was in ancient China. At first, the Chinese poured hot water onto powdered tea. From the 1200s, they added hot water to dry tea leaves, often in a teapot, let them steep (soak), and then strained out the leaves. Today most people just use tea bags. The tea bag was invented in 1908 by Thomas Sullivan of New York. He would often send samples of tea to his customers in small silk bags. Some people mistakenly thought the whole thing was to be placed in hot water rather than just emptying out the tea leaves. No problem! The tea bag had accidentally been invented. However, it wasn't until the 1970s before the British decided that using a tea bag was

Today, most people use tea bags. However, in ancient China, the tea leaves may not have been strained out. In fact, during later dynasties, tea leaves were dried into a powder and stirred in.

acceptable. Until then, using tea leaves in a teapot and a strainer was the "proper" way to make tea and similar to the way the ancient Chinese did it!

OODLES OF OLD NOODLES

Do you and your family ever eat takeout? Many of us eat noodles as part of Chinese meals or dishes such as mac and cheese. Pasta and noodles are some of the most popular foods today.

The process of making noodles involves a flour mixture made into dough, which is then pulled into strips and boiled. The oldest noodles discovered (at the Lajia archaeological site) were very thin and yellow, much like China's popular la mian—a traditional pulled noodle.

Historians originally thought that pasta was invented in the Middle East. But in the early 2000s, workers found long, thin yellow noodles made from a grain called millet in a sealed bowl at the Lajia archaeological site in northwestern China. The noodles have been dated to 4,000 years ago, so some historians now think the inventors of noodles were the ancient Chinese. Noodles are very difficult to make even today, so the find showed how skilled the ancient Chinese were.

FACT

People in the West came up with the term "noodle" for long, thin pasta. In China, a noodle is called "miàn" or "mein." That name isn't based on the shape of the food but the fact that it is produced from flour in a liquid.

The stretchy la mian noodles were traditionally pulled about 3 feet (1 meter) long. They symbolized long life during the Chinese New Year.

FOOD AND FARMING IN ANCIENT CHINA

Early Chinese people lived in the valley of the Yellow River. The land there was fertile and easy to farm. The dry climate meant that millet was a simple crop to grow. Other groups of people lived near Hangzhou Bay. The climate there was useful for growing rice. Wet rice farming started about 5000 BC.

Farmers' lives were not easy. Most jobs on farms were done by hand, so it meant a lot of hard work. Threshing, hoeing, and spreading manure took a lot of time and effort to carry out. Using the irrigation systems that ensured crops had enough water was another big task. Farmers had to pay a tax to the emperor and also had to give a large part of their crops to their landlord. This meant that sometimes the farmer's family had little left for themselves.

WHAT'S NOT TO LOVE ABOUT RICE?

Bored of sandwiches for lunch? Rice bowls are a new easy-to-make lunchtime meal. Mixed with meat, beans, or vegetables, these bowls are becoming more and more popular. Where does rice come from originally? You guessed it! China. Rice has been farmed there for thousands of years. It was a staple of the Chinese diet. Rice needs a lot of water to grow, so the Chinese worked to improve irrigation methods in order to provide all that water. The land was flooded to form paddy fields. Books written between 475 and 221 BC included discussions about farming rice. The way that rice was farmed is still very similar today.

Rice was grown primarily in the south of China. It was harvested and used to make wine, cakes, and puddings.

INTRODUCING CHOPSTICKS!

When you eat Chinese takeout, do you use chopsticks? Well, you probably won't be surprised that chopsticks were invented by the ancient Chinese.

About 5,000 years ago, chopsticks were used for cooking. They were probably just twigs that were dipped into large pots of boiling water to remove food. But by about AD 400, the population had increased. The ancient Chinese needed to save fuel. One way was to chop food into very small pieces so that it cooked faster. Knives were then no longer needed after the food was cut, so a different tool was invented—chopsticks! Then people began to use them for eating. They were made mainly from bamboo, but also ivory, animal bones, or porcelain were used.

About 5,000 years ago, chopsticks were used for cooking.

FACT

Emperors used silver chopsticks because they thought they would change color if someone had poisoned their food! Of course, this wouldn't always have been helpful. Some poisons do not cause silver to change color, and some ordinary foods, such as onions, do.

CHAPTER 4

SPARKLING SMILES AND HEALTH

Today, Chinese medicine is trusted by many as either an alternative to Western medicine or to use alongside it. More than 10 million acupuncture treatments take place every year in the United States alone.

ACUPUNCTURE—THE GOOD KIND OF NEEDLES!

How would you feel if someone started sticking needles in your body and telling you not to worry because it will cure your headache? It seems like a strange idea, but acupuncture is used by some people to relieve pain and improve general health. Thin needles are placed at certain points on the body in order to heal problems such as arthritis, asthma, and migraines; and to help the flow of energy around the body.

Acupuncture was developed by the ancient Chinese almost 4,000 years ago. It is based on the idea that people

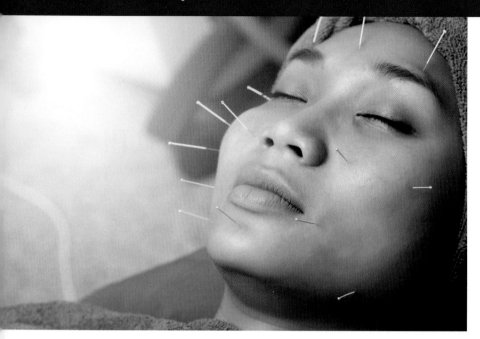

become ill when the body is not in balance. The body needs to be reset in order to make a person well again. Yin and yang—the dark and the light—are the two sides of every person. There are channels (also known as meridians) around the body in which Qi (life force) flows.

The first mention of acupuncture appears in *The Yellow Emperor's Classic of Internal Medicine*, dating from about 100 BC. During the Ming dynasty (1368–1644), *The Great Compendium of Acupuncture and Moxibustion* was published. This is the basis of modern acupuncture. In it are descriptions of hundreds of points on the body. These points represent openings to the channels in which needles could be placed to alter the flow of Qi.

In ancient China, acupuncture needles were probably made of stone or animal bones. Ouch! Later, bamboo was used, or sometimes gold or silver. Nowadays, the needles are usually made from stainless steel.

In the past, acupuncture was viewed as a scam in the Western world. But, over the years, scientific studies have shown that acupuncture can be helpful in relieving pain and fighting disease.

HYGIENE AND MEDICINE

Hygiene was very important to the ancient Chinese. Around 500 BC, gentlemen were to wash their hands five times a day and wash their hair every third day. They only had to bathe every five days, though!

The ancient Chinese system of medicine focused on the body being balanced. Herbs and plants were used to treat all kinds of problems, and they still are. The ancient Chinese also knew that eating food after heating it and boiling water before drinking it would make it safe.

WHAT WOULD YOU DO WITHOUT YOUR TOOTHBRUSH?

What are you supposed to do twice a day for two minutes at a time? Brush your teeth! Bristle toothbrushes like those we use today were invented by the Chinese.

Variations of the toothbrush have been around for thousands of years. Chew sticks—or twigs with frayed ends that were rubbed on the teeth—had been in use from about 3500 BC. However, it was 1498, during the Ming dynasty, when Emperor Hongzhi patented the bristle toothbrush. Coarse hair from the back of a pig's neck was used for the bristles and bamboo cane or bone for the handle.

A TOOTH BROOM?: MASS PRODUCTION AND DEVELOPMENTS

Around 1780, William Addis, a rag merchant, was in a London prison. He made himself a toothbrush after being inspired by a broom! He found a bone on the floor, got some boar (pig) bristles from one of the guards and the toothbrush was created! Once out of prison, Addis began selling horsehair toothbrushes in London. He was the first to mass produce toothbrushes. They became popular after the introduction of sugar from the West Indies. Not surprisingly, there were a few more decayed teeth around!

H. N. Wadsworth got the first U.S. patent for a toothbrush. He declared that he had improved the toothbrush's design by separating and angling the bristles more so that they could reach between the teeth more efficiently. The Addis company in the UK supplied toothbrushes to soldiers during World War I to help them develop the habit of cleaning their teeth. This was the same company that had been created by William Addis in the late 1700s.

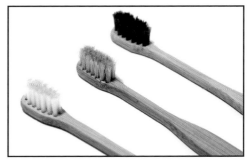

Bamboo handles and horse hair bristles made up one kind of toothbrush available. In 1938, an artificial material called nylon was used to make toothbrush bristles. However, tooth brushing still didn't really take hold in the United States until after World War II, when soldiers brought the habit home with them.

Today all kinds of different styles and sizes of toothbrush are available. These include electric (the first of which was made in 1939), battery powered, soft bristles, and medium bristles. But the basic style of bristles on a handle remains the same as the ancient Chinese version patented by Emperor Hongzhi.

FACT

In 2003, a survey asked people which inventions they couldn't live without. The list of items included the car, computer, mobile phone, microwave, and toothbrush. But out of those things, the toothbrush was the number-one invention!

CHAPTER 5

SILKY SECRETS: HOME AND GARDEN

What fabrics are your fanciest clothes made out of? Do you have any dishes at home that you only use on special occasions? From the fanciest to dirtiest of occasions, you might already be familiar with some of the ancient materials and inventions for use at home for work or play. The ancient Chinese were responsible for many inventions that can be found in and around our homes.

SILK OF LEGENDS

Raising silkworms (actually the caterpillar of a type of moth) for the production of silk is called sericulture. Silk is a high-quality material used for clothes and furnishings among other things. It is good for regulating temperature, so it is used for top-quality bedding and nightwear. Silk keeps people warm in winter and cool in summer.

Legend has it that Emperor Huangdi's first wife, Leizu, discovered how to produce silk and then taught it to others. The story is that Leizu was drinking tea in the garden, under a mulberry tree. A silkworm cocoon dropped from the tree into her tea. The cocoon split, revealing lengths of silk thread up to 3,300 feet (1 kilometer) long. Leizu began to breed and raise silkworms. She fed them mulberry leaves because it was soon discovered that those produced the best silk. The cocoons also needed to be dropped into boiling water before they hatched in order to produce the most silk. It is believed that Leizu even invented the loom in order to weave the silk thread into fabric.

Silkworms form cocoons that are made of one long strand of silk. The strand can measure 1,000 yards (915 meters) long. The domestic silkworm moth species is no longer found in the wild.

However, no one knows exactly when silk was first made, but a recent archaeological find suggests that silk dates back 8,500 years. Archaeologists have explored tombs at Jiahu in central China. Two tombs had evidence of silk, perhaps from clothing worn by people buried there. Archaeologists also found weaving tools. Silkworm breeding may have taken place in the area, partly because the climate there is perfect for mulberry trees.

A MEASURE OF PAYMENT AND STATUS

Silk was used as a form of payment during the Tang dynasty. It is thought that the cost of things could be measured by lengths of silk. Some farmers were known to pay their taxes in silk and grains.

During the Han dynasty (2nd century BC), silk became one of the main exports from China along the Silk Roads to Rome, Italy. It was highly valued not just by the Chinese but also by wealthy Europeans.

The types of clothing worn by the rich and poor in ancient China differed greatly. Silk was worn only by the wealthiest and most important people. Even merchants who traded in silk were not allowed to wear it. If it was discovered that someone was wearing silk underneath their outer clothing, they were punished. It was the Qing dynasty (1644–1912) before everyone was allowed to wear this luxurious fabric. That was assuming they could afford it, of course!

SILK ROADS

The Silk Roads were nearly 7,000 miles (11,300 km) of trading routes from China to the Mediterranean Sea. The name "Silk Road" wasn't used until geographer Baron Ferdinand von Richthofen used that term in 1877. China began to trade with western Asia and Europe around 112 BC. Silk wasn't the only item traded, though. Spices, tea, metals, glass, and paper were also traded.

IT'S A SECRET!

Silk production was a closely guarded secret by the ancient Chinese. It was around 200 BC before Korea found out about it, and it was even later before other people found out about it. Two visiting monks had smuggled a silkworm inside a walking stick. They took the silkworm to the Byzantine Emperor Justinian I and the secret was out. But it was after 1200 AD before silk production began in Europe.

FACT

The Romans called China Serica, meaning "Land of Silk."

Today silk has come full circle. It is mainly a luxury item because more and cheaper artificial materials have been developed in the last century.

PORCELAIN: GRANDMA'S BEST CHINA

So, come on, own up. Have you ever broken a dish at home? Who hasn't?! Today we take porcelain for granted, but we might not have it at all if it weren't for the ancient Chinese. It is used for all kinds of dishes, plates, and vases. High-quality porcelain is also known as china because it originally came from China! Many families have older members who keep their "best" china for special occasions.

A basic form of porcelain was produced during the Han dynasty (206 BC–AD 220). However, porcelain–similar to what we know today–was first created during the Yuan dynasty (1279–1368). This true (or hard-paste) porcelain is made from petuntse (a rock) that is ground into a powder. It is then mixed with kaolin (also known as white china clay) and heated to such a temperature that it becomes glass-like.

Kaolin is a white clay that is soft and can be molded after it is mixed with water. It is used for making many types of products including porcelain. It is named for the place in China where it was mined—a hill called Kao-ling.

THE PORCELAIN CAPITAL OF CHINA

Have you ever been at your grandma's house and been served on a fancy blue and white plate? This type of porcelain originally comes from China. It was perfected during the Ming dynasty (1368–1644), which is famed for its amazing arts and crafts. After they defeated the Mongols in 1368, the Chinese began to increase the production of porcelain. They used a form of assembly line production where each worker took on a separate task, such as shaping the porcelain or painting it. Workshops were set up at Jingdezhen in Jiangxi province. This is an area where there is a plentiful supply of suitable clay and stone. Enough porcelain could be made to satisfy demand in China and export to other countries.

Blue and white china was prized for its color—the ingredient used for the blue color was often hard to get. The color was made with cobalt, which was brought to China via the Silk Roads. During some periods, blue-and-white porcelain was reserved for special occasions or used for diplomatic gifts.

Europeans did not discover how to make porcelain in the same way as China until 1707. Beginning in the 1500s, they had been making what is known as soft-paste porcelain. Bone china was mixed with bone ash in a version of the hard-paste porcelain made in China. Josiah Spode the Second, an Englishman, developed bone china around 1800.

Bone china is popular in the UK and the U.S., while most of Europe prefers hard-paste porcelain. Porcelain is now used not just for tableware but also for tiles, jewelry, and even bathtubs!

WOODEN GOATS, AKA WHEELBARROWS

Wheelbarrows are commonly used in gardens, on building sites, and anywhere else a heavy load needs to be moved. You will probably remember learning about them at school as simple machines with levers and the wheel and axle.

Well, wheelbarrows are a Chinese invention. Legend has it that in the first century BC, inventor Ko Yu built "a wooden goat" to ride away on!

SECRET WEAPON WHEELBARROWS

Chuko (Jugo) Liang was the ruler of Shu Han, one of the Three Kingdoms that followed the Han dynasty. Supposedly, he was the real inventor of the wheelbarrow. During a military campaign, his enemies tried to starve

his army. But he produced a "secret weapon" that could easily carry rations and other supplies along narrow trails because there was only one wheel, not two.

Over the years, the ancient Chinese developed ways the wheelbarrow could be used. Sometimes, people would sit in the wheelbarrow and be pushed from place to place. One version from the 1700s even had sails to harness the wind!

FACT

The Chinese called the wheelbarrow a "wooden ox" or a "gliding horse."

43

EUROPEAN WHEELBARROWS

The first image of a wheelbarrow in the West was on a stained-glass window in Chartres Cathedral, in France, dated around 1220. The wheel was further toward the front of the box than in the Chinese version.

During the 1600s, traders traveling through China brought back news of the Chinese version of the wheelbarrow. It soon became popular in Europe.

By 1706, the wheelbarrow was seen as being perfect for gardening. It was mentioned as a "necessary" tool in Francis Gentil's book of 1706, *Le Jardinier Solitaire* (The Solitary or Carthusian Gardener). Now, any serious (or not so serious!) gardener owns a wheelbarrow. Thanks to that ancient Chinese invention, people no longer need risk injuring themselves when lifting a heavy load!

GO FLY A KITE

Have you ever taken a kite out on a windy day and watched it soar through the sky? It's a popular pastime for many families.

About 2,500 years ago, a philosopher named Mo Di, or Mozi (468–376 BC), lived in China's Shandong province. He made a wooden bird in the shape of an eagle and managed to keep it flying in the air for a day before it broke. He taught his pupil, Lu Ban, how to make it. Lu Ban suggested using bamboo because it weighed less than wood. His kite stayed airborne for three days.

The first kites made were called *muyuan*, meaning "wood kite." Later, paper was used for making kites. Then the name changed to *zhiyuan*, which means "paper kite." Today, the most common name for a kite in China

Modern kite design hasn't changed much since ancient times. The materials may be different, but they still use the same methods to fly!

is *feng zheng*. *Feng* means "wind" and *zheng* is a traditional, wooden string instrument similar to a zither. People began to attach thin strips of bamboo to their kites, which made a sound that was like that made by the zheng instrument.

LEISURE IN ANCIENT CHINA

As well as kite flying, the ancient Chinese played card games and board games such as Go. The Chinese called it *weiqi*. Weiqi is a game of strategy that is still played today. The Chinese played a sport similar to polo and even invented an early form of soccer, called *cuju*, around 200 BC. Music, dancing, acrobatics, and shadow-puppet plays were popular types of entertainment. Festivals were also common, such as the Lantern Festival and the Dragon Boat Festival.

KITES JOIN THE MILITARY

By AD 100 kite flying was a common pastime in China. Kites have been used for a number of practical purposes. These include weather vanes for testing wind direction, and in the military for measuring distance and sending messages. It is thought that kites with messages were flown over Mongol battle lines by the ancient Chinese from about 1232. The kites landed among the Chinese prisoners, encouraging them to escape. Possibly the most famous kite user was Benjamin Franklin. His kite experiment in 1752 was carried out in order to demonstrate a connection between lightning and electricity.

Chinese kites took on the shapes of dragons and animals as shown in a colored engraving from 1843. Throughout the centuries since its invention, the kite has brought people together to enjoy the outdoors.

Hundreds of years after its invention, kite flying is still a form of entertainment for many, not just in China but around the world. It has been developed into other sports too, such as kiteboarding and hang gliding. Kite making is still seen as an art in China. Designs on kites often include Chinese characters meaning happiness or good luck. Along with its uses in war and for research, the invention of the kite has given us many reasons to be thankful to Mo Di and Lu Ban.

BROLLY, RAINSHADE, BUMBERSHOOT, ROBINSON, OR UMBRELLA?

No matter what you call them, people of many different countries use umbrellas. Most umbrellas sold around the world are made in China. That includes the more than 33 million sold in the United States each year. Today, Songxia, China, is thought to be the biggest umbrella-making city in the world. More than 1,000 companies make about half a billion umbrellas each year.

Umbrellas are essential for rainy countries like the United Kingdom, but they are also used to protect people's skin from the sun in hot climate countries. In fact, that was the reason that the umbrella (or parasol) was originally invented about 4,000 years ago. Evidence of these types of umbrellas have been found in several ancient civilizations, including China and Egypt. But it was the Chinese who first waterproofed their umbrellas.

Oil paper umbrellas first appeared during the Han dynasty (206 BC–AD 220). They were made from bamboo and thin paper made from tree bark. The umbrellas were covered in tongyou, a plant oil that comes from the tung tree, to make them waterproof. They were not just used for keeping the owner dry. They were works of art. Decoration in the form of birds or flowers were painted on before the oil was applied. Some people in China still make these umbrellas and claim that they should be able to withstand winds of over 20 miles (32 km) per hour.

In the 1700s, Jonas Hanway popularized the umbrella in the United Kingdom. He saw them used during his travels throughout Russia and the East, including China. In the West, umbrellas had mainly been seen as fashion accessories for women.

Bamboo cane ribs were replaced by whalebone and then steel. A folding umbrella was patented in 1969 by Bradford Phillips, an American. There have also been pocket umbrellas, huge golf umbrellas, and even umbrella hats!

FACT

Robinson Crusoe, a character in the 1719 novel by Daniel Defoe, was the fictional inventor of the umbrella. Later in the 1700s, when umbrellas became more common in the United Kingdom, they were nicknamed "Robinsons."

CHAPTER 6

BOOMING INVENTIONS

The ancient Chinese were responsible for so many inventions! The following are just a few more that deserve to be highlighted.

DRAWN TO THE RIGHT PATH: THE MAGNETIC COMPASS

As the forerunner of Global Positioning System (GPS) devices and still used by people who like to go hiking, the compass is helpful in finding your way. But it's changed a bit over time.

Around the 4th century BC, the lodestone compass was used by the ancient Chinese. It helped them ensure that they build their houses in a direction that would lead to harmony in their lives. It was also used for fortune-telling. Lodestone, a form of the mineral magnetite, is a natural permanent magnet. It aligns itself

The spoon-shaped compasses used during the Han dynasty (206 BC–AD 220) were placed on a plate divided by straight lines. The circle in the center represented heaven and the square represented earth. Points on the plate were related to constellations, and diviners would often use the compass to tell the future.

with Earth's magnetic field. A spoon-shaped compass, known as a "south-pointer," was used during the Han dynasty.

These early compasses were used to find the south, not the north. A manuscript called *Wu Ching Tsung Yao*, written in 1040, has a mention of "an iron fish" that pointed to the south when suspended in water. The Chinese had discovered a way of magnetizing an iron needle by rubbing it with magnetite. The earliest mention of such a magnetic device used for telling direction appeared in a book written between 1040 and 1044 during the Song dynasty.

Development of the compass was vital for trade, especially for ships carrying cargo. Compasses appeared in Italy around the beginning of the 1300s. But it was the English that worked on making improvements as so much of their trade was based on sea routes. It was an advantage to be able to navigate with something other than the stars.

Of course, now we have GPS to help direct us where we want to go. GPS uses connections to satellites in space to find locations. Wouldn't the ancient Chinese be impressed by that?

GUNPOWDER PLOTS AND ALCHEMISTS

U.S. Independence Day, Guy Fawkes Night, and many other celebrations around the world would be very different without the invention of a certain black powder by the ancient Chinese. Gunpowder has had a massive effect on our lives. Not only is it used in fireworks, but also in weapons. Its invention completely changed how wars are fought. The Chinese invented guns, rockets, bombs, and landmines.

Gunpowder was originally created by Chinese alchemists around AD 850. The aim of these men was to discover a tonic of immortality, or the chance to live forever.

Saltpeter (another name for potassium nitrate) was readily available in China. It was a whitish crust that could be found on some soils. Alchemists had experimented with it for many years. Mixed with sulphur and charcoal, this resulted in a black powder that caused the alchemists' hands to be burned. The black

Gunpowder is an explosive substance. Today a smokeless powder is usually used in weapons, but the black powder is still used for fireworks and certain ammunitions.

powder came to be known as *huo yao*, or "fire drug."

FIREWORKS FROM THE FIRE DRUG

In AD 1110, the Chinese army put on a display of fireworks for the emperor. It was described in an ancient text called *Dreams of the Glories of the Eastern Capital*. Early fireworks were simply gunpowder in bamboo sticks. They were set alight and aimed at the sky. The noise was likened to thunder. And if you can imagine it against the darkness of night without electricity lighting the cities and towns, the fireworks would have looked spectacular. Also, there would have been a lot of smoke from the gunpowder.

Fireworks were popular in Europe by the 1400s. At the wedding of Anne Boleyn and King Henry VIII in 1533, gunpowder was used in a huge display that included a "great red dragon that spouted out wild fyre." In 1613, during a performance of Shakespeare's

play *Henry VIII*, gunpowder was used for realism. Unfortunately, sparks set the thatched roof on fire and the theater burned down. Luckily, no one was hurt, but one man's pants caught fire. Someone emptied a bottle of ale on them to extinguish the flames!

Later developments included adding metal filings to produce brighter sparks. Mixing in coarsely ground charcoal created floating sparks. In the 1800s, adding the salts of different metals led to much more colorful fireworks.

WEAPONS OF MAGIC FIRE

The Chinese military quickly realized the possibilities of gunpowder for weapons. The first explosive bombs were used more to frighten or startle the enemy than cause injury or death. In the 1200s, during the Song dynasty, the army used gunpowder in various weapons against the invading Mongol army. It didn't do them much good, though, because the Mongols won the war and established their own dynasty, the Yuan.

In the late 1200s, Chinese military technicians developed the gun. At first, it fired stones and cast-iron balls. Cannons were also developed. Both were commonly used in battle by 1359.

The earliest written reference to gunpowder in Europe is in a 1242 letter from the English scientist and philosopher Roger Bacon to the Pope. Less than 100 years later, in 1337, gunpowder was being used by King Edward III in the war against France. Reports told of iron bullets being shot forth by fire: "They made a sound like thunder." Just a few decades after that, guns were regularly being used in warfare. Of course, guns are still in use around the world today and not just in war zones.

FACT

The ancient Chinese had some very inventive names for bombs, including the "Bandit-Burning Vision-Confusing Magic Fire-Ball" and the "Bone-Burning and Bruising Fire Oil Magic Bomb" (which contained porcelain shards, iron pellets, oil, urine, and feces)!

WAR

In the 500s BC, a book called *The Art of War* was written by Sun Tzu (Master Sun). It described battle tactics. Until the invention and use of gunpowder in weapons, war had been the strength of one man versus another. Swords, spears, and even battering rams and catapults all needed human muscles to work. Gunpowder changed things. It meant there was a need to develop new battle tactics as well as new training methods. Therefore a new type of soldier emerged.

A SEISMOGRAPHIC INVENTION

Are there earthquakes where you live? A seismograph is an earthquake detector. It records the motion of the ground. In areas of the world where earthquakes can cause major damage and loss of life, the importance of the seismograph can't be understated. Today, earthquakes are predicted and detected through hi-tech gadgets. The original idea came from Chinese philosopher Zhang Heng in AD 132.

It is thought that Zhang Heng's seismoscope was unable to predict earthquakes but it could show what direction they came from. The instrument was a large jar with eight metal dragons placed around it, at major compass points. Eight open-mouthed metal toads were placed underneath each dragon head. If there was an earthquake, a ball would drop from the mouth of the dragon facing in the direction of the earthquake. The ball would land in the toad's mouth. The Emperor would then know, at least roughly, where to send help.

If there was an earthquake, a ball would drop from the mouth of the dragon facing in the direction of the earthquake.

Scientists are not quite sure how the detector worked or exactly what it looked like. But it probably involved a pendulum inside the jar. The pendulum was sensitive to vibrations in the earth. An earthquake would move the pendulum, which would activate a lever. The lever would force one of the dragons to release its ball into the toad's mouth.

The machine supposedly once detected an earthquake 400 miles (644 km) away! A messenger from a village that was 400 miles away arrived not long after the seismograph had detected the earthquake and confirmed the machine's result.

Today, earthquakes are detected and recorded by extremely sensitive equipment. Rather than using a pendulum, seismographs use a large permanent magnet. The outside of the seismograph contains many coiled

wires. When the magnet moves, electrical signals in the wires are sent to a computer, or recorded on paper, as a seismogram. Scientists can make predictions for when an earthquake is likely to happen by studying readouts recorded by seismographs at different places. That all sounds very impressive, doesn't it? But, let's be honest, Zhang Heng's seismograph would have been much more interesting to look at!

A BIG IMPACT

The ancient Chinese invented many items that have had a great impact on history and on the world we live in today. Some of these inventions have been further developed with modern technology, but we still owe their introduction to the ancient Chinese. Think about how vital paper and printing have been in educating people around the world. Trade improved once the magnetic compass was invented. And wouldn't you miss that nice glass of iced tea on a hot day? These are just some of the reasons we should care about the ancient Chinese!

THE END OF THE ANCIENT CHINESE CIVILIZATION

In 1911, a number of revolts broke out in China. These were led by a man known as Sun Yat-sen. With support from the military and from the provinces, he declared China a republic on January 1, 1912. The last emperor, 6-year-old Puyi, had to give up his role as a result. Some historians argue that "ancient" China ended many centuries before, at the end of the Han dynasty around AD 220.

GLOSSARY

civilization—an organized and advanced society

civil service—government jobs

culture—group of people's way of life, ideas, customs, and traditions

dynasty—ruling family

(the) East—countries located east of Europe and North and South America, such as China, Japan, and India

export—send and sell goods to other countries

font—a set of letters and symbols in a particular design

mass production—making an item in large quantities in order to sell it

merchant—person who sells or buys goods in large amounts

military—armed forces

patent—the right to be the only one to make, use, or sell an invention for a certain number of years

philosopher—person who studies ideas, the way people think, and the search for knowledge

republic—political system in which officials are elected to represent citizens in government

Silk Roads—routes across both land and sea, along which silk and other goods were traded

smuggle—move something secretly and often illegally

tax—money or goods that people give to the government in order to help pay for public services

(the) West—located in or relating to Europe and North and South America

ADDITIONAL RESOURCES

Read More

Cottrell, George. *The Shang Dynasty*. New York: KidHaven Publishing, 2017.

Howell, Izzi. *Explore! Ancient China*. London: Wayland Publishing, 2016.

Samuels, Charlie. *The Shang and Other Chinese Dynasties*. London: Franklin Watts, 2015.

Steele, Philip. *Children's Encyclopedia of Ancient History*. Chapel Hill, NC: Armadillo Books, 2019.

Internet Sites

The British Museum: Ancient China
www.ancientchina.co.uk/menu.html

BBC: Shang Dynasty Class Clips
www.bbc.com/bitesize/topics/z39j2hv/resources/1

DK Find Out!: Ancient China
www.dkfindout.com/uk/history/ancient-china

SELECT BIBLIOGRAPHY

Burbank, Jane and Frederick Cooper. *Empires in World History: Power and the Politics of Difference.* Princeton, NJ: Princeton University Press, 2010.

Clark, Josh, "Top 10 Ancient Chinese Inventions," HowStuffWorks, March 9, 2009, https://science.howstuffworks.com/innovation/inventions/10-ancient-chinese-inventions1.htm Accessed August 26, 2019.

Cottrell, Arthur. *Eyewitness: Ancient China.* New York: Dorling Kindersley, 2005.

Delbanco, Dawn. "Chinese Calligraphy," The Met, April 2008, https://www.metmuseum.org/toah/hd/chcl/hd_chcl.htm Accessed August 26, 2019.

Hansen, Valerie. *The Silk Road: A New History.* New York: Oxford University Press, 2012.

Kelly, Jack. *Gunpowder: Alchemy, Bombards, and Pyrotechnics: The History Of the Explosive that Changed the World.* London, UK: Atlantic Books, 2004.

Liyao, Lin, "Top 10 Greatest Inventions of Ancient China," China.org.cn, March 4, 2011, http://www.china.org.cn/top10/2011-03/04/content_22054243_10.htm Accessed August 26, 2019.

"Porcelain," Encyclopædia Britannica, February 12, 2019, https://www.britannica.com/art/porcelain Accessed August 26, 2019.

"Silk," Encyclopædia Britannica, March 7, 2019, https://www.britannica.com/topic/silk Accessed August 26, 2019.

Sivasubramaniam, Sinnathurai, "Tea," Encyclopædia Britannica, March 22, 2019, https://www.britannica.com/topic/tea-beverage Accessed August 26, 2019.

"Top 20 Ancient Chinese Inventions," USC US-China Institute, 2019, https://china.usc.edu/sites/default/files/forums/Chinese%20Inventions.pdf Accessed August 26, 2019.

About the Author

Claire Throp has been working in publishing for more than 20 years. She has written more than 60 nonfiction books for children on subjects such as British history, sports, biographies, wildlife, and countries. She lives in the UK.

INDEX